Words I Never Spoke

Warren Theroux

Presentation by *BookLeaf Publishing*

Web: www.bookleafpub.com

E-mail: info@bookleafpub.com

ISBN: 9789395756327

First edition 2022

DEDICATION

To my shag-eared villain, my mysterious hamlet, the one who fucks verily,

For I know all and I know best.

C.C.C.D.

ACKNOWLEDGEMENT

Thank you for being here,
Supporting me,
Loving (or hating) my words.
I appreciate all that everyone does for Me,
Good or bad.
It's more than I deserve, truly.
I wish I could do more for you guys,
Instead of just writing down some words,
Maybe making you guys giggle or feel less alone.
Although, those are pretty good things.
I just wish I could do more.

PREFACE

Trigger warning
This contains mentions of suicide, abuse, drug
use, mental illness and toxic relationships.

Sbubby

You mean so much to me,
You always have.
The idea of someone ever caring for you never
has even graced your pretty little brain,
For you are the forgotten.
Left behind by anyone and everyone,
And regretfully,
Me.
Although I realised I had lost a diamond,
And raced to get you back.
You came happily along,
Like I had never left you alone in the rain
Starving and broken.
I will never be worth you,
Nothing I can do will ever repair the damages I
caused you,
The pain others have caused you that I wasn't
there to heal you from,
To protect you from.

Teacher

It was never easy,
Before I met you.
Everything had to be fought for tooth and nail
and it made me wonder if any of it was worth
the effort.
I know now that it was.
You made it worth it.
All of the fights and arguments with every
person I saw
The countless hours of abuse
Deteriorated mental health that kept going
downhill because no one seemed to care enough
to do anything about it you,
Kept me here.
Made me see that I wasn't the only person that
needed help.
You opened my eyes to a world that didn't
criticise me and put me down when I was
already buried in the ground.
While everyone else was drowning me,
You handed me your raft and said,
"Time to float."

You pulled me to shore and dried me in your
seaside shack.

A place that has taught me that a disaster can
still be beautiful,
A little home that had no right to be as such.
My favourite times are when it's in the afternoon
and the sun hits just right and comes through the
big windows.
You can see every single little particle of dust,
Aimlessly floating.
It is then, that it feels right to be there.
You never felt that way.
It was only me.
You always stood and smiled
Letting me have my few moments of peace.
You knew that I needed that time.

You don't want to be here.
Yet you're still here.
You're leaving soon and you're leaving me
afloat.
Hoping that I can do this on my own.
I don't think I will,
But I'll try.
I'll make my life better if only out of spite
Not to you, but to everyone else that thought of
me worthless.
You taught me worth.

Why?

Why you care about me is well beyond my
comprehension.
I am basically a child for you to take care of.
You don't deserve that,
No one does.
I've never been important to anyone else,
Besides you of course,
And I never understood why.
Now I question,
Why do you care?
Why do I,
A person of comprised of anxiety and attitude,
Someone you care so deeply for
That you would care if I left?
I am nobody,
Just another human that takes up space,
Someone that has no worth or meaning.
I just burden you,
A waste of your time,
Space,
Energy.
You shouldn't be friends with me,
You don't deserve to be weighed down by me.

Beeblebub

5

I always thought,
Happiness,
Was a person reading a book in the corner,
sipping jasmine tea,
Laundry in the corner folded neatly,
While it shines outside,
With jazz softly in the back.

I now realise,
Happiness,
Is a person giggling at my stupidity, slightly
buzzed off wine,
Landing on the long forgotten pile of laundry in
the corner,
While it is rains outside,
With bassy trap music in front.

Firefighter

You soothe my anger,
Fingers brushing over my cheeks the same water
does over fire,
My temper sizzles and eventually fades.
The only thing left now is a crumbling pile of
tears and sobs of apology.
Yet you still stand,
Looking over the ruble I've created and holding
out your hand.
You help me rebuild what I've destroyed.

Wordless

7

Have you ever gone to write something,
But nothing you wrote was good enough?
I've tried to write the same thing twenty times,
Yet nothing seems to hit just right,
No string of words can quite form what I want to
say.
I guess that's the thing about love,
There are no words to describe it,
Only feelings.

Ex-Muse

What am I supposed to do?
You're no longer the topic of my muse,
No longer do you hold the title for my love.
Your name strays far,
Your voice refuses to linger,
Not a singular part of you occupies my brain,
You're now just a distant memory.
Something I never thought I could accomplish,
I thought I would love you forever,
Convinced that you were impossible to get over.
Alas, here I am.
Over you.

Odd Notion

My heart no longer aches when I think of you.
An odd notion, truly.
After four years,
I am finally,
f i n a l l y ,
Over you.

Te Amo, Mi Amor

There's not a single moment that made me fall in
love with you,
Just as there is no one thing.
It's a collection of both.
When you stood up for me the first time,
When you gave me a hug and I cried.
The way you squeak when you sneeze,
Or say "sshhhiiiit" after you yawn like an old
man.
When we watched a movie together and you just
stared at me,
Watching my eyes reflect the scenes.
The way you let me hold your arm when we're
in public.
All of these things helped me fall in love with
you,
And I willingly took the plunge.

My Dearest Friend

The day I asked for you,
You came,
As quickly as you left.
You got down on your knees,
Pleading,
Begging,
For me to never send you away again.
I told you to stand up,
To never get on your knees for anyone ever
again,
You're worth more than that.

True Crimes

It's a crime truly,
How you stole my heart.
You're like a thief in the dark,
Scurrying away from the scene,
Never to be seen again.
Aloof during the day,
Mischievous at night.

All My Wishes

13

I wish for one thing in my life:
To not fuck up.
Alas, Over and over again,
I fail myself.
This is why I don't wish for you.
Because if I lost you,
That would be the biggest mistake of my life.

Haha, I kill me

Some days,
I wish we still had each other.
Sitting in your attic high and bleeding,
An addiction I never realised I had until it was
gone.
Other days,
I wish we had never been.
Not being able to call you when I needed
release,
That was the hardest thing to let go.
Alas,
Here I am,
Over you and our situationship,
Clean in every way.
Sometimes,
The pang of loss hits me,
And I miss it.
I almost dial your number after a bad day,
Because I still have it memorized,
Along with all the episodes of Alf we watched.
I still have your face etched into my brain,
Mostly from the countless hours I started at you.
You are still so pretty,
Even after you killed me.

Bug Bites

15

Being an addict is like having a bug bite.
You don't like the fact you have one,
It's itchy and ugly,
Everyone knows you have a bug bite.
But its almost worth having one when you
scratch it.
That feeling of pure bliss and euphoria tingling
up your skin,
Hitting parts of your brain your brain you didn't
realise you had.
It makes having a bug bite a luxury for ten
seconds.
That's all it takes to want to have another one.
Just another line,
Hit,
Drink.
Just once more scratch.

Self Gaslighter

Do you think they really care?

What do you mean?

Won't they just replace you when you're not
needed? You're just useful to them now, a tool
for future success.

Why would you say that? They've given me no
reason to think this.

Yes they did. When they left you for other
friends at a con, when they forgot to buy you
food but remembered everyone else. You're
useless to them. Nothing but a burden.

I'm a burden?

You're a burden, not just to them, but to
everyone. How many people have forgotten
about you? Gone months without talking to you?
Only ever used you for their benefit?

Everyone.

That's right. You're going to be replaced by everyone. No one wants you around unless you're useful, and you're not. It's a matter of time. You're going to be alone forever.

I'm going to be alone forever?

Forever. Until death at best.

So I'm a burden, no one truly cares about me, and I'm going to die alone?

Correct.

I'm a burden, no one truly cares about me, and I'm going to die alone. I'm a burden, no one truly cares about me, and I'm going to die alone. I'm a burden, no one truly cares about me, and I'm going to die alone. I'm a burden, no one truly cares about me, and I'm going to die alone. I'm a burden, no one truly cares about me, and I'm going to die alone.

Remember Maybe?

Do I have what it takes to be remembered?
I know I'm too scared to ask questions,
Or form a sentence when people talk to me,
Or hold eye contact for more than three seconds,
But is my intelligence enough,
Or the way I word things or pronounce things
Enough for someone to remember me?
I know I'm a two on a twenty scale physically,
But I'm really smart.
I can't talk though,
Nor do I like being around people.
I'm an introvert with chronic social anxiety and
autism,
So I'm lucky if I'm even noticed.

Forgotten Again

Do you enjoy forgetting about me?
It seems like every single time I have to rely on
you,
You're never there.
In any situation.
Always late by hours, if you even bother to
show.
Do you just not care?
Am I not worthy enough for you?
I know I wasn't the best person to be around,
But I've grown, I'm better now.
Am I still as worthless as the day I was born?

First Generation Fuck Up

Why can I never do anything right?
I always seem to fuck up somehow,
Nothing I ever do is good enough.
Does everyone else have this problem?
Is it just me?
Am I so broken that I am causing my own issues
and not realising it?
I used to think it was me against the world,
Now I think it's me against myself.
I'm my own obstacles.
Maybe I need to get rid of myself,
That's what I supposed to do, right?
Get rid of the obstacles,
Even if it hurts me?

Monster, monster

21

I want a monster to be friends with.
But my bed sits on the floor,
Leaving no monster room to hide.
I just want someone to care about me as much as
my anxiety does.
I want someone to be as clingy as my
depression.
I just wish someone would enjoy having me
around,
Alas,
No one wants to deal with me.
I get it,
I'm too much.
I'll just stay over here then,
Looking for a monster to become friends with.

Dry drowning

The feeling of drowning is back.
With tenfold force as to last time.
I need to breathe but I can't reach the surface.
I'm trying to breathe but water keeps rushing in
my lungs but I'm above water, I'm in my bed,
Why do I still feel this way if I'm in my bed,
I need to reach the surface,
I'm kicking
Screaming
Nothing is working nothing at all
Maybe if I just sit , I'll float to the top.
Maybe then I'll be dead and I won't have this
feeling anymore.

Thank you

23

Can I write you something?
It's a thank you,
For supporting me.
For reading.
For the comments (good and bad).
I'll try to make this short and sweet,
Strawberry.
Wait, that's a long word.
Sugar.
Yeah, sugar.
Short and sweet.

www.ingramcontent.com/pod-product-compliance
Lightning Source LLC
LaVergne TN
LVHW021719210726
843509LV00021B/2857